POLDARK'S CORNWALL

Gill Knappett

PITKIN

POLDARK:
THEN AND NOW

When Winston Mawdsley Graham penned his first *Poldark* novel, *Ross Poldark*, in the 1940s, it is unlikely that he could have imagined that he would still be writing about the character over 50 years later. But such was the popularity of the novels that in 2002, just a year before the author died, the twelfth and final book in the Poldark series, *Bella Poldark*, was published.

Born Winston Grime in Manchester in 1908 – he later changed his surname to Graham by deed poll – he moved with his parents to Perranporth in Cornwall when he was 17. The author's first novel, *The House with the Stained Glass Window*, was published in 1934, and eleven more followed before *Ross Poldark* was published in 1945.

The *Poldark* adventures are set against a backdrop of the dramatic Cornish coast of the late 18th and early 19th centuries, with the first tale beginning in 1783, when Captain Ross Poldark returns to Cornwall from the American Revolutionary War. So begins a family saga of romance, jealousy, betrayal, feuds, intrigue and tragedy.

LEFT: Winston Graham in 1985

ABOVE: Aidan Turner as Ross Poldark

The novels, which first captured the imagination of post-war Britain, went on to be translated into over 30 languages. An adaptation of the first seven books for television in the 1970s proved highly popular, and in 2015 the BBC brought *Poldark* to life once more, introducing the characters to a 21st-century audience. The 2015 series averaged over eight million viewers per episode, and several further series of the period drama followed.

As a result of *Poldark*'s on-screen success, actor Aidan Turner (Ross Poldark) has become a household name. Few can forget the image of him in the famous scythe-wielding scene, and at the National Television Awards in 2016 he was presented with the 'Impact Award' for his performance. Other leading roles have been played by Eleanor Tomlinson as Ross's wife, Demelza;

Heida Reed as his first love, Elizabeth; and Jack Farthing as the man who became his arch-enemy, the ruthless financier George Warleggan.

But, of course, there is a much bigger star of the show: Cornwall. In *Poldark's Cornwall* we take a trip around the most south-westerly county in England – many parts of which are now in the care of the National Trust – exploring the beautiful locations used for filming the series as we follow in our fictional hero's footsteps. Travelling from the historic harbour of Charlestown and heading along the sheltered south coast, circling the gaunt headland of mainland Britain's most south-westerly point, then along the breathtaking north shoreline with its crashing, Atlantic waves, and on to the bleak beauty of Bodmin Moor, we hope that you will enjoy the journey.

THE SOUTH

CHARLESTOWN

The historic port of Charlestown, with its iconic tall ships, has been a popular filming location for *Poldark*. It not only stood in for the towns of Truro and Falmouth – the latter the home of Captain Andrew Blamey (actor Richard Harrington) and from where he and Verity Poldark (Ross's cousin, played by Ruby Bentall) elope in series one – but its beach became St Mary's in the Isles of Scilly, where, in series two, Ross Poldark seeks out the fugitive Mark Daniel (Matthew Wilson), a miner who killed his wife, Keren (Sabrina Bartlett), after discovering she had been unfaithful to him with Dr Dwight Enys (Luke Norris).

Charlestown was originally called West Polmear, a tiny fishing village where its handful of residents made a living from catching pilchards. Its fortunes changed when the entrepreneur Sir Charles Rashleigh built a port here between 1791 and 1801 in response to the region's expanding mining industry; the village and port were subsequently renamed Charlestown in his honour. Originally used for exporting copper, Charlestown later became important for the export of china clay from local quarries when the material was discovered in Cornwall in the early 18th century.

Today Charlestown – a UNESCO World Heritage Site – remains a fine example of a Georgian port, retaining much of its character from that period.

Aidan Turner as Ross Poldark in Charlestown

CHARLESTOWN SHIPWRECK AND HERITAGE CENTRE

Charlestown's Shipwreck and Heritage Centre is built over the tunnels through which dock workers transported wagonloads of china clay to the ships moored in the port.

The displays here tell the story of the commercial activity and trade generated by the building of Charlestown, and the growth, and eventual decline, of its industry. Here too is a unique insight into the thousands of shipwrecks that have taken place off Britain's shores, with stories of courage, cowardice, triumph and tragedy.

TURNAWARE POINT

West of Charlestown, and on the Roseland Peninsula side of the River Fal, not far from the harbour-side village of St Mawes, is Turnaware Point. It is famed for being an embarkation point for the D-Day landings of 1944 but for *Poldark* fans it became a location in France for covert landings in series three. During this series, Dr Enys – who first met Ross Poldark during the American Revolutionary War and later moved to Cornwall – is imprisoned in France but is subsequently rescued by Ross and a raiding party.

Sunrise over Charlestown harbour

THE LIZARD

The Lizard Peninsula is a 20-mile or so stretch of coast, where emerald seas meet beautiful beaches nestled far beneath the clifftop path. The awe-inspiring Lizard Point, in the care of the National Trust, is mainland Britain's most southerly point, whilst inland are heather-covered downs, pretty woodlands and the village of Lizard – the name meaning 'high place' in Cornish. The Spanish Armada is said to have been first spotted from here in 1588.

Smuggling is an important part of Cornish history, and the Lizard's sheltered coves – some of which feature in *Poldark* – were well used by those bringing in contraband. But the hazardous coast was also the location of many shipwrecks and looting from wrecks was accepted as part of a Cornishman's lot, apart from with the authorities.

LIZARD LIGHTHOUSE HERITAGE CENTRE

In 1619, Sir John Killigrew funded the building of a beacon tower on Lizard Point, an unpopular move with the locals who said he was 'taking away God's grace' from them and the Lizard's first lighthouse was demolished a few years later. It was not until the 1750s that the support of Trinity House – dedicated to safeguarding shipping since 1514 – saw a twin-towered building erected. In 1998 the lighthouse was automated. Today visitors can visit the lighthouse, climb to the top for magnificent views and explore the Heritage Centre with its interactive displays.

The lighthouse at Lizard Point is an iconic landmark on the South West Coast Path

KYNANCE COVE

Hidden amongst the cliffs of the Lizard is Kynance Cove. The long walk down from the carpark is worth the effort for the sheltered beach with white sands, rock pools and interconnecting caves. These can be explored at low tide – but visitors should beware the strong currents and know that at high tide the beach disappears.

Kynance Cove has been used for several beach scenes in *Poldark*. Here, at the end of series one, Ross is arrested for wrecking, inciting a riot and murder, and marched off to Truro jail. It is also the backdrop for the clifftop riding scene in the opening sequence of series two. In that same series, Kynance Cove becomes Nampara Cove, where the heavily pregnant Demelza sets off alone in a fishing boat; Ross wades into the water and rescues her when she gets into difficulties and goes into labour. In an interview, Aidan Turner said that when filming the scene a huge wave lifted the boat and slammed it into him, causing him to drop Demelza into the sea, which he was first to admit was 'not very Ross Poldark'.

MULLION COVE

A four-and-a-half-mile walk along the coast brings you to Mullion Cove. Whilst *Poldark* fans will not see this small, sandy cove in the TV drama, it was at the Mullion Cove Hotel, overlooking Mullion Harbour, that the cast and crew stayed when filming nearby. However, close by, at Predannack Wollas, both Ross and Demelza rode the windswept headland on horseback.

The working harbour at Mullion was completed in 1895, financed by Lord Robartes of Lanhydrock to help local fishermen who had suffered several disastrous pilchard seasons. Half a mile offshore is the uninhabited Mullion Island, owned by the National Trust and a breeding ground for seabirds.

POLDARK MINE

On the Lizard Peninsula is Helston, where the Polkdark Mine visitor attraction is on the site of a mine originally known as Wheal Roots. Some of the underground mine scenes in *Poldark* were filmed here.

GUNWALLOE

A few miles north of Mullion Cove is Gunwalloe, which lays claim to being the first Cornish entry in the Domesday Book. Nestled amongst the sand dunes – a few steps from the golden shore of the aptly named Church Cove – is the tiny medieval church of St Winwaloe, where Dwight Enys and Caroline Penvenen (Gabriella Wilde) are married in *Poldark* series three. The building's close proximity to the often tempestuous sea led to its nickname, 'The Church of the Storms'.

Just yards away is Jangye-ryn, more generally known as Dollar Cove because of the silver coins that have been washed ashore over the years. Several ships which have come to grief here may have supplied the treasure, including a Spanish galleon carrying silver dollars in 1786 and a Spanish brig in 1802, which the *Sherborne Mercury* reported 'was coming from Malaga with dollars, gold, and silver plate and fruit'.

ABOVE: Wildflowers on the cliffs at Dollar Cove

RIGHT: St Winwaloe's Church at Church Cove

HENDRAWNA BEACH
Dollar Cove became the fictional Hendrawna Beach at the end of series one of *Poldark*. This is where Ross sees Warleggan's ship, the *Queen Charlotte*, being tossed onto rocks in the stormy sea and rushes to gather the villagers so that they can collect the beached cargo.

THE WEST

LAND'S END

The westernmost tip of Cornwall is the peninsula known as Land's End, which stretches from Penzance on the south coast to St Ives on the north coast; between these two points are many locations with *Poldark* connections.

Land's End itself is one of Britain's most famous landmarks and has been attracting tourists for over three centuries. As well as myriad activities at the Land's End Visitor Centre, there are around 100 acres of breathtaking landscape in this designated Area of Outstanding Natural Beauty.

PENBERTH COVE

A few miles east of Land's End is the tiny fishing haven of Penberth Cove, with its distinctive stone cottages, large stepping stones bridging the stream and the slipway leading to a pebbled beach.

Penberth appears regularly in *Poldark*, becoming Sawle village and home to Demelza's brothers, Sam and Drake Carne (actors Tom York and Harry

Richardson), in series three. The slipway stars many times – including in series two when Ross Poldark's manservant, Jud Paynter (Phil Davies), is seen on it, intoxicated and singing. The stepping stones here also feature, crossed by several of the characters at various times.

ABOVE: *Cottages and stepping stones at Penberth Cove*

LEFT: *Tom York as Demelza's brother, Sam Carne*

PEDN VOUNDER

With its crystal-clear waters and white sands, Pedn Vounder – a naturist beach – is increasingly sought out as a destination, despite a steep climb down from the clifftop path. In *Poldark*, Pedn Vounder and the neighbouring Porthcurno Beach (the two meet at low tide) feature as Nampara Cove when Ross and Demelza walk over the sands towards Treryn Dinas on the headland in a dream sequence.

PORTHCURNO

The stunning bay of Porthcurno is the setting for many beach scenes in *Poldark*. Its white sands, turquoise waters and freshwater stream make it ideal for families, and you may be lucky enough to spot dolphins out at sea.

As well as its beauty, Porthcurno is famous for two other things: the Minack Theatre and the Telegraph Museum.

BELOW: Pedn Vounder with Treryn Dinas, an Iron Age promontory fort, on the right

RIGHT: Minack Theatre

TELEGRAPH MUSEUM

Porthcurno was the starting point for the world's first underwater telegraph cable, laid beneath the Atlantic Ocean in 1866; by the 1930s all telegraph communications linking the British Empire to such faraway lands as the United States, China and South Africa passed below the beach here. Today the Telegraph Museum, through exhibitions and interactive displays, illustrates the important part Porthcurno played in the history of international communication. Indeed, so important was the communication centre here that its telegraph station was moved underground during the Second World War, and visitors can explore the bomb-proof tunnels that were dug into the hillside.

MINACK THEATRE

Built into the cliffs and overlooking the sea is this amazing amphitheatre, accessed via the beach or by road. In the early 1930s a local drama group was looking for a venue to perform *The Tempest*. Rowena Cade decided to create a setting for the play in the grounds of her home, Minack House, and with the help of her gardener set to work, moving boulders and building terraces. The success of the Shakespeare production in 1932 encouraged Rowena to continue developing this open-air theatre, and today the 750-seat auditorium hosts a marvellous summer season. The Exhibition Centre here tells the full story of the Minack Theatre and visitors can also enjoy the sub-tropical gardens in this magical spot.

PORTHGWARRA

Walking west along the South West Coast Path from Porthcurno for just over a mile – or a 10-minute drive by road – brings you to picturesque Porthgwarra, England's most south-westerly cove. The slipway here gives a clue to Porthgwarra's heritage as a once-busy fishing hamlet. Next to the slipway are entrances to tunnels cut by tin miners from nearby St Just. Although some say the tunnels were used by smugglers, one was created to give access to the horses and carts of farmers who collected seaweed to fertilise their fields; the other gave access to 'hulleys', built into the rock for fishermen to store shellfish before they took them to market. In *Poldark*, one of the tunnels is where Ross keeps his boat, which, in series one, Mark Daniel uses as a means of escape after murdering his wife in a fit of rage after learning of her infidelity.

Also in series one is the 'pilchard scene', where Ross and Demelza, along with other men and women from the community, come to the beach to fill their baskets from boats that have landed huge

CORNISH SARDINES

The export of Cornish sardines – another name for pilchards – was first recorded in 1555 and for centuries the annual harvest of these fish was important to fishing villages. A good catch meant families could preserve and sell them, and store some for themselves, but would face starvation if the pilchard season proved a poor one.

numbers of the fish, which, as Ross says, 'will make a difference this winter'.

But perhaps most memorable of all, it is from the clifftop at Porthgwarra that Demelza sneaks a secret glimpse of Ross swimming naked in the sparkling waters.

BELOW: Ross Poldark kept his boat in one of the tunnels in the cliffs at Porthgwarra

GWENNAP HEAD

A short distance from Porthgwarra is the rugged, rocky headland of Gwennap Head. This stunning part of the Cornish coastline which features in the background many times in *Poldark* – including in series four when Ross bids farewell to Demelza and their children as he heads off for London to pursue a career in Parliament – is reportedly one of Aidan Turner's favourite filming locations.

Gwennap Head is a great place to see wildlife, including dolphins and porpoise, even whales, and numerous species of seabirds. It is, however, one of the UK's most dangerous stretches of water. The building of Wolf Rock Lighthouse, nine miles out to sea, was completed in 1869, although several navigational markers had previously been placed on the notorious rock from which the lighthouse takes its name.

A National Coastwatch station is based at Gwennap Head, opened in 1996 and replacing the coastguard station which closed two years previously. The station is part of the National Coastwatch Institution, run by volunteers who

TOP: *A carriage scene filmed at Gwennap Head*

ABOVE: *A brooding Ross Poldark in series four*

keep watch along various sections of the UK's coastline. One of the things the watchkeepers here look out on is the infamous Runnel Stone Reef, which has been the site of several shipwrecks.

ST JUST

St Just-in-Penwith, to give it its full name, is proud to be England's most westerly town and was once the centre of the tin mining industry on the Land's End peninsula. The town retains its character, with granite cottages lining the narrow streets, and disused engine houses and chimney stacks dominating the landscape. The stretch of coastline here was known as 'The Tin Coast' and in the 19th century there were over 100 engine houses – used to raise ore and pump water out of the mines – in the district of St Just. Two of the mines, Botallack and Levant, feature in *Poldark*.

St Just is a charming place to potter, with shops and galleries displaying the work of local artists, and a lovely parish church, the current building dating from the 15th century. Close to the church is Plain-an-Gwarry, an amphitheatre or 'playing place', where miracle plays were performed in medieval times.

Every July, the town celebrates Lafrowda Week, a community arts festival, with outdoor events which culminate in the grand finale, Lafrowda Day.

BOTALLACK AND LEVANT MINES

Around one-and-a-half miles north of St Just are the Botallack Mines, and a mile further on is Levant Mine and Beam Engine, both National Trust sites. The engine houses of these mines were built in their spectacular cliffside positions when mining in Cornwall was at its height.

BOTALLACK

Botallack, part of the Cornish Mining World Heritage Site, is an important part of the county's mining history; it closed in 1895 due to falling tin and copper prices.

In *Poldark*, as well as providing an impressive panorama for several clifftop scenes, the abandoned buildings of two of the real mines here – Wheal Owles and Wheal Crowns – became the fictional Wheal Leisure, Grambler and Wheal Grace, and were used for external filming (the internal shots taking place at the Poldark Mine visitor attraction near Helston).

In series two, Ross is forced to sell his shares in Wheal Leisure to George Warleggan, but opens Wheal Grace in partnership with his cousin, Francis Poldark (actor Kyle Soller).

RIGHT: Filming a mining scene

BELOW: Atlantic waves crash onto the rocks below Botallack Mine

MINING TRAGEDY

In *Poldark* series two, Francis tumbles into the water and drowns at Wheal Grace. Sadly there was a real-life tragedy at Wheal Owles; when it was a working mine in the 19th century, floodwater trapped some of the miners underground. *The Cornishman* newspaper of 12 January 1893 reported: '19 men and a boy died in the watery darkness of Wheal Owles, at St Just-in-Penwith. A terrible roar was heard by the 40 men and boys working deep underground ….' The bodies of the 20 who lost their lives were never recovered.

LEVANT MINE AND BEAM ENGINE

Levant is home to the only still-working, steam-driven beam engine. In *Poldark*, the buildings become Tressiders Rolling Mill, where copper from the Poldark family mine is processed. Here in series two, Ross and Francis are seen debating claims by the engine's inventor, Richard Trevithick, about the machine's capabilities.

BELOW: Levant Mine and Beam Engine

RIGHT: Kyle Soller as Francis Poldark

WHAT'S IN A NAME?
As many of Cornwall's mines are prefixed by the word 'wheal', it is often thought that it is Cornish for 'mine', but in fact it means 'place of work'.

ST IVES MUSEUM

The St Ives Museum is housed in a building that was used for pilchard-curing in the 18th century, before becoming, at various times, a laundry, cinema and a hotel for shipwrecked sailors. The museum displays a variety of collections relating to the life and times of the town and county in general.

LEFT: Art exhibition in Tate St Ives

ST IVES

St Ives is the last town on the north coast of the Land's End peninsula. Its working harbour, sandy beaches and maze of narrow streets, lined with whitewashed fishermen's cottages and Victorian terraces, create a quintessentially Cornish scene.

There is a special quality of light here and it is no surprise that the town has been attracting artists since the early 19th century. As a result, there are numerous artists' studios and art galleries in the town, the most famous being Tate St Ives which opened in 1993 in recognition of the international importance of art in Cornwall and in particular St Ives .

A short walk from Tate St Ives is the Barbara Hepworth Museum and Sculpture Garden. Yorkshire-born Barbara Hepworth, one of the most influential sculptors of the 20th century, moved to St Ives in 1949 with her husband, Ben Nicholson. Trewynn Studios – now the museum – was her home until her death in 1975.

On the upper reaches of the town is The Leach Pottery. Bernard Leach – often referred to as 'the Father of British studio pottery' – established a pottery here in 1920, and today the studio, museum and gallery celebrate his work and influence on the development of ceramic arts.

The North

~❧~

ST AGNES

Chimneys and engine houses crowd the cliffs of St Agnes Head, reflecting its tin- and copper-mining past, and the sweeping views proved the ideal setting for the *Poldark* family estate, Nampara Valley, when filming the drama.

At one time there were over 100 mines in the parish and its terraced granite cottages were once miners' homes. The steep lane called Stippy Stappy is referred to in Winston Graham's books, in which St Agnes itself becomes the fictional village of Sawle. This slope features in series two of the television series when Prudie Paynter (Beatie Edney) threatens to knock her husband Jud 'sideways down Stippy Stappy lane'.

Today the village shops and galleries, selling local produce and artworks, are popular with visitors, as is the St Agnes Museum. Full of artefacts and information charting the history of the area, the museum is described as a 'cabinet of curiosities'. It also has a self-portrait of one of St Agnes' most famous sons, the artist John Opie (1761–1807), who became a professor at the Royal Academy and is buried next to Joshua Reynolds in St Paul's Cathedral, London. Opie is mentioned in series two of *Poldark* when George Warleggan tells Elizabeth, now his wife, that he is commissioning a

CHAPEL PORTH

Both St Agnes Beacon – well worth the climb for stunning panoramic views – and the ruins of Wheal Coates overlook Chapel Porth, west of St Agnes village, where a vast beach is exposed at low tide. The clifftop here is seen regularly in *Poldark* when Aidan Turner, as Ross, gallops along it.

portrait of the two of them to replace the one of her previous husband, the late Francis Poldark.

St Agnes is close to a number of beaches. The one nearest the village centre is Trevaunance Cove; its rock pools and caves are much enjoyed by families, and its relatively calm sea is popular with those learning to surf. At low tide, the ruins of the harbour from which ore from the mines was exported can be seen. A little inland from Trevaunance Cove, at Trevellas Coombe, is Blue Hills Tin Streams. This is a family-run business and visitor centre where craftspeople produce gifts and jewellery using tin harvested from this stretch of coastline under special licence from the Duchy of Cornwall.

BELOW: Trevaunance Cove

BELOW LEFT: Jack Farthing and Heida Reed as George and Elizabeth Warleggan

ABOVE: St Agnes' Stippy Stappy lane

PERRANPORTH

With three miles of golden sands washed by the Atlantic's waves, and sand dunes rich in wildlife, Perranporth is one of Cornwall's' most glorious beaches. In *Poldark* it becomes Hendrawna Beach and appears in many scenes in the televised drama, including romantic encounters between Dwight Enys and Caroline Penvenen, the wealthy heiress who the doctor eventually marries.

Perranporth was author Winston Graham's home for many years and he served as a coastguard here during the Second World War. Graham lived in the town – his own house was called Nampara Lodge, the name Nampara also given to Ross Poldark's estate – until 1960 and it is where he wrote the first four Poldark novels: *Ross Poldark*, *Demelza*, *Jeremy Poldark* and *Warleggan*. He named one of Poldark's mines Wheal Leisure, after a tin mine in Perranporth that closed in the 20th century.

ST PIRAN

There are many saints connected with Cornwall. St Piran is not only one of its patron saints but also patron saint of tin mining, and St Piran's Day is celebrated throughout Cornwall in March each year. It is St Piran that Perranporth is named for: legend has it that he was cast over the sea from Ireland, a millstone round his neck, and washed up on the coast here. He went on to found St Piran's Oratory on nearby Penhale Sands; once buried by sand, its remains were excavated in the 19th century and again in 2014. St Piran's Cross – one of the earliest recorded stone crosses in Cornwall, mentioned in a charter of AD 906 – is located near the oratory.

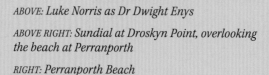

ABOVE: Luke Norris as Dr Dwight Enys

ABOVE RIGHT: Sundial at Droskyn Point, overlooking the beach at Perranporth

RIGHT: Perranporth Beach

Although he moved from Cornwall in 1960, Winston Graham retained close connections with his adopted home town and was president of its Perranzabuloe Museum until his death. The collections in the museum provide a fascinating account of the life and history of the parish from the earliest times, whilst special exhibitions showcase new acquisitions and cultural developments over the centuries.

DROSKYN POINT

Below the cliffs at Droskyn Point – at the southern end of Perranporth Beach – historic mines have been exposed by coastal erosion.

A huge granite sundial was installed on the clifftop here to celebrate the millennium. Its hours are marked by standing stones, aligned to show 'Cornish time' which is 20 minutes ahead of Greenwich Mean Time.

HOLYWELL BAY

Halfway between Perranporth and Newquay – one of Cornwall's biggest towns – is the mile-long beach of Holywell Bay. Its sweeping shoreline backed by towering sand dunes, through which a stream meanders down to the sea, makes this a wonderful place for families, and at low tide the wreck of an old ship can be spotted offshore.

The iconic twin peaks of Gull Rock (also known as Carter's Rock) mean Holywell Bay is instantly recognisable to *Poldark* fans as the Warleggans' beach in series two. Holywell Bay beach itself is foregrounded many times in the drama, especially as a romantic setting: Ross and Demelza are seen strolling here; Dwight Enys and Caroline Penvenen ride on horseback as waves break on the seashore; Drake Crane and Morwenna Chynoweth (Ellise Chappell) have a liaison on the beach; and Demelza has a secret rendezvous with Lieutenant

Hugh Armitage (Josh Whitehouse). It is also here that, in the opening scenes of series four, Ross emerges from the ocean; in a later episode, Demelza plays on the sand and paddles in the shallows with her children.

A HOLY WELL

A well in Holywell Cave – a destination for pilgrimages made by parents with sick children – is likely to have given the bay its name. Calcium deposits in the cave have created a grotto-like appearance; the cave is accessible from the beach at low tide but nevertheless visitors are advised to only explore with caution.

TRERICE

Just three miles inland from Newquay is Trerice, the elegant manor house that was the inspiration for Trenwith in Winston Graham's novels. Trenwith, the home of Ross Poldark's uncle and cousins, is central to the stories, although Chavenage House in Tetbury, Gloucestershire is where filming of the television series took place.

Trerice is at Kestle Mill, reached via narrow, leafy lanes so synonymous with Cornwall. This beautiful Elizabethan manor house, in its tranquil setting, has changed little since the early 1570s when the Arundell family, whose family seat it had been since the 14th century, began building the house seen today.

In 1953 Trerice House and its grounds were purchased by the National Trust. The house had fallen into disrepair but its tenant, John Elton, turned it into a comfortable family residence.

A visit to the house provides an opportunity to appreciate its history and reflect on the lives of the people who lived here. Trerice's gardens are delightfully intimate and include a formal knot garden, planted in Elizabethan style; a parade ground – used by Newquay's Home Guard unit during the war – and lawn where visitors can enjoy picnics and games. The mowhay, a field dedicated as a natural habitat for wildlife, has a maze, created in 2018, which invites visitors in to explore the area.

LEFT: A view of Gull Rock from Holywell Bay

BELOW: There is much for visitors to enjoy at Trerice

PORTHCOTHAN

A little north of Bedruthan Steps is the pretty beach of Porthcothan, another location which becomes Nampara Cove. On the southern edge of Porthcothan bay are the tiny Trescore Islands; at low tide, an azure lagoon is formed which provided the venue for some swimming scenes in *Poldark*.

BEDRUTHAN STEPS

Situated between Newquay and Padstow are Bedruthan Steps, another exciting backdrop in *Poldark*, especially when Ross gallops his horse along the clifftop, but the view is also seen in series four just before the funeral of baby Sarah Enys takes place.

Bedruthan Steps are actually three huge rock stacks, named for the giant of Cornish legend who is said to have used them as stepping stones to cross the bay.

For anyone not choosing to make the steep climb down to Bedruthan Steps – and visitors should be aware that it is unsafe to swim here – a breathtaking view can be enjoyed from the precipice at Park Head. It is along Park Head, with Bedruthan Steps in the background, that

ABOVE: Caroline Enys (Gabriella Wilde), cradles her baby on the beach in series four

BELOW: Bedruthan Steps

ABOVE RIGHT: The harbour at Padstow

Demelza is seen walking in series two. In the same series, Dwight Enys is filmed riding at Park Head, on his way to meet with Ray Penvenen (John Nettles), who wants the doctor to stop pursing his niece, Caroline.

Separating the beach at Bedruthan Steps from Pentire Steps Beach is Diggory's Island, although at low tide the two beaches join to form one long stretch of sand. It is at Pentire Beach that, in *Poldark* series four, Dwight and Caroline meet up with Ross and Demelza.

STEPPER POINT

The peninsula of Stepper Point – part of the Prideaux-Brune family estate – overlooks Padstow bay and provides the thrilling backdrop in *Poldark* when horse-drawn carriages are featured racing along the clifftop. It is also here that, in series three, the heavily pregnant Elizabeth Warleggan struggles to control her horse; as it bolts towards the headland, Ross comes to the rescue. In the background, waves are seen crashing on the inlet known as Butter Hole.

PADSTOW

Padstow, a traditional fishing harbour situated on the Camel Estuary, was also once a major port when local mining and quarrying industries were flourishing. Padstow Museum is full of artefacts, documents and photographs charting the long history of the town. Although the fishing industry is still important here, Padstow has evolved to become a very popular tourist destination, not least of all with those wishing to dine at one of Rick Stein's famous seafood restaurants.

There are several lovely beaches in close proximity and fantastic walks to be enjoyed in the surrounding countryside. The town is also the starting point of the Camel Trail, an 18-mile cycle route in three main sections along a disused railway: Padstow to Wadebridge; Wadebridge to Bodmin; Bodmin to Wenfordbridge.

May Day in Padstow is celebrated with the 'Obby 'Oss festival which welcomes spring and is linked to ancient fertility rites. Crowds process as two 'obby 'osses dance through the streets in an attempt to catch young maidens. The celebrations end at midnight, with a song that signifies the death of the 'obby 'oss and its resurrection the following May.

PRIDEAUX PLACE

A short walk from Padstow harbour is Prideaux Place, home to the Prideaux-Brune family. It was Sir Nicholas Prideaux who built the house on land formerly owned by the Prior of Bodmin. The mansion was completed in 1592 and the same family has lived here ever since. Additions and alterations were made by successive generations in the 18th and 19th centuries, and an on-going restoration programme ensures it is not only a charming family home but one that is greatly enjoyed by visitors.

The house is an elegant mix of Elizabethan and 'Strawberry Hill' Gothic and the fine collections of furniture, porcelain, paintings, photographs and memorabilia form an inspiring insight into Cornish life through the centuries.

Much work has been carried out to restore the magnificent 40-acre grounds to their former glory, with the remodelling including a Victorian

formal garden. Here too is a deer park. Watching the fallow deer being fed is a great draw for visitors, and the animals can even be viewed from the comfort of the tearoom which overlooks the deer park and enjoys fabulous views over the Camel Estuary.

POLDARK AND PRIDEAUX PLACE

Winston Graham was a great friend of the Prideaux-Brune family and a regular visitor to their home. Prideaux Place is often referred to in the *Poldark* books: the house is visited by Ross Poldark and in *Bella Poldark*, the final book in the series, Graham introduced a new character: Captain Philip Prideaux.

THE EAST

BODMIN MOOR

The River Tamar forms the Devonshire/Cornish boundary and a few miles from the border is one of the best-known parts of east Cornwall: Bodmin Moor.

Bodmin Moor's vast, desolate landscape, punctuated with granite tors, gives it a wild, romantic character, perfect for filming *Poldark*. It is used as the setting for miners' cottages, including the one lived in by Jim and Jinny Carter (the characters played by Alexander Arnold and Gracee O'Brien). Ross Poldark is very fond of the young couple and tries to help them by allowing them to live there rent-free.

WARLEGGAN

On Bodmin Moor is the hamlet of Warleggan, after which Winston Graham named one of the most significant families in his *Poldark* books.

LEFT: *Prideaux Place*

BELOW: *Wild ponies on Bodmin Moor*

ST BREWARD

Around 15 miles inland from Padstow, and on the western edge of Bodmin Moor, is the village of St Breward. Its name derives from St Branwalader, patron saint of the parish church. Standing 700 feet (213m) above sea level, this is thought to be highest church in the county.

Within the parish of St Breward are two even higher landmarks: Brown Willy (or Bronn Wennili, Cornish for 'hill of swallows') and Rough Tor. At 1,378 feet (420m) above sea level, Brown Willy is the highest point in Cornwall, and Rough Tor second at 1,313 feet (400m). Both landmarks are seen in the background in *Poldark* series two, when Ross gallops across the moorland, heading for Bodmin to await trial, accused, amongst other things, of the murder of George Warleggan's cousin, Matthew, whose body was washed ashore following the shipwreck at the end of series one.

Perhaps most significant of all is the privately owned farmhouse near St Breward which takes

ABOVE: Dr Dwight Enys's cottage

ABOVE RIGHT: Aidan Turner as Ross Poldark in series two

RIGHT: Bodmin Jail

centre stage, externally at least, as Ross Poldark's cottage at Nampara. St Breward is also the location of Dwight Enys's cottage.

BODMIN

The town of Bodmin, approximately 10 miles south of St Breward, is steeped in history and has much to offer visitors, including Bodmin Town Museum, Cornwall's Regimental Museum and, just outside the town, the National Trust's beautiful Lanhydrock estate, with its Victorian country house and gardens set in 900 acres of parkland. Familiar to *Poldark* fans, of course, is Bodmin Jail.

BODMIN JAIL

Bodmin Jail was first built in 1779, and replaced in 1850 with a new prison which closed in 1927. Bodmin was the site of many executions and in 1909 the last hanging inside the jail took place. During the First World War the prison walls housed some of the nation's treasures, including the Crown Jewels for a short period.

The jail is where Jim Carter, in *Poldark* series one, is incarcerated for poaching, despite Ross's efforts to save his young employee from a prison sentence. Later, after learning that Jim is seriously ill – the result of a deadly pestilence sweeping through the jail – Ross and Dr Enys attempt to rescue him but unfortunately the young man does not survive the ordeal.

It is also Bodmin Jail where Ross is locked up in series two, before being found 'not guilty' of crimes linked to the shipwreck at the end of series one.

In 2018, work started to transform the former jail – said to be one of the most haunted places in Britain – into a new visitor attraction and education centre, with a luxury hotel on the site of this Grade II-listed building.

MINIONS

On the south-east side of Bodmin Moor is Minions, the highest village in Cornwall and a great base for exploring the moors. Minions Heritage Centre is accommodated in an engine house which once served the South Phoenix Mine, portraying the importance of the area as an industrial centre in years gone by. The volume of mining and quarrying in the 19th century created the need for a railway, evidence of which can still be seen at nearby Cheesewring Quarry.

Walk just a couple of miles beyond Minions to discover a wealth of sites of archaeological interest, including the ancient standing stone circles known as The Hurlers, and The Cheesewring. The Hurlers, managed by the Cornwall Heritage Trust on behalf of English Heritage, are three stone circles dating

RIGHT: The Cheesewring, so named because it is shaped like a press used in traditional cheese-making

BELOW: The Hurlers; in the background is Minions Heritage Centre, situated in an old engine house

ABOVE: Crossroads on the characterful, evocative Bodmin Moor

from around 1500 BC and named for the men who, legend has it, were turned to stone for playing the game of hurling on the Sabbath. The Cheesewring is a distinctive towering natural rock formation, where granite slabs rest on top of each other.

It is at the crossroads at Minions that, in *Poldark* series one, the dashing Captain Poldark alights from the carriage as he returns to Cornwall from the American Revolutionary War, before making his way to visit his uncle, Charles Poldark (actor Warren Clarke), and cousins at Trenwith. His happy homecoming, however, is thrown into turmoil when he discovers that the woman he hoped to marry is now promised to another. And so begins the tale ...

THE COPPER TRAIL

Minions is a popular starting point for this 60-mile circular walking route around Bodmin Moor. The trail provides a varied landscape of moorland, granite tors, farmland and wooded valleys; it passes through hamlets, villages and towns – including St Neot, Bodmin, Blisland, St Breward, Camelford and Altarnun, where the parish church is known as 'The Cathedral of the Moors'. There are many disused copper mines to be seen along the way, reflecting the heritage of the area and giving the trail its name.

POLDARK'S CORNWALL

Atlantic Ocean/
Celtic Sea

Bude

Launceston

Stepper Point

Prideaux
Place

Bodmin
Moor

St Breward

Minions

Porthcothan

Padstow

Wadebridge

Bedruthan
Steps

Bodmin

Liskeard

Saltash

Holywell Bay

Newquay

Lostwithiel

Droskyn Point

Looe

Penhale Sands

Trerice

Torpoint

Perranporth

St Austell

Fowey

Chapel Porth

St Agnes

Charlestown

Botallack Mine

Truro

Levant
Mine

Redruth

Turnaware
Point

St Ives

Camborne

Hayle

Falmouth

St Mawes

English Channel

Penzance

St Just

Helston

Land's End

Dollar
Cove

Penberth
Cove

Mullion
Cove

Pedn
Vounder

Gunwalloe
Church Cove

Porthcurno

Kynance Cove

Lizard

Porthgwarra

Gwennap
Head

N

W   E

S